Fergie Jenkins

THE STORY OF THE TEXAS RANGERS

Second baseman Rougned Odor

THE STORY OF THE

TEXAS
RANGERS

JIM WHITING

Nolan Ryan

CREATIVE EDUCATION / CREATIVE PAPERBACKS

Published by Creative Education and Creative Paperbacks
P.O. Box 227, Mankato, Minnesota 56002
Creative Education and Creative Paperbacks are imprints of The Creative
Company
www.thecreativecompany.us

Design and production by Blue Design (www.bluedes.com)
Art direction by Rita Marshall
Printed in China

Photographs by Alamy (Cal Sport Media, Ron Jenkins/Fort Worth Star-
Telegram/MCT, Richard W. Rodriguez/Fort Worth Star-Telegram/TNS, UPI), AP
Images (ASSOCIATED PRESS), Corbis (Bettmann), Creative Commons Wikimedia
(The Sporting News Archives), Getty Images (Al Bello/Allsport, B Bennett,
Lisa Blumenfeld, Bruce Bennett Studios, PAUL K. BUCK/AFP, Chris Covatta/
Allsport, Jonathan Daniel/Allsport, Diamond Images, Stephen Dunn/Allsport,
Focus on Sport, Otto Greule/Allsport, Paul Jasienski, Bob Levey, Brad Mangin/
MLB Photos, National Baseball Hall of Fame Library, Christian Petersen, Rich
Pilling/MLB Photos, Louis Requena/MLB Photos, Rick Stewart/Allsport, Tony
Tomsic/MLB Photos, Jared Wickerham)

Library of Congress Cataloging-in-Publication Data
Names: Whiting, Jim, author.
Title: Texas Rangers / Jim Whiting.
Series: Creative sports. Veterans.
Includes index.
Summary: Encompassing the extraordinary history of Major League Baseball's
Texas Rangers, this photo-laden narrative underscores significant players,
team accomplishments, and noteworthy moments that will stand out in
young sports fans' minds.
Identifiers: ISBN 978-1-64026-321-5 (hardcover) / ISBN 978-1-62832-853-0
(pbk) / ISBN 978-1-64000-451-1 (eBook)
This title has been submitted for CIP processing under LCCN 2020901768.

First Edition HC 9 8 7 6 5 4 3 2 1
First Edition PBK 9 8 7 6 5 4 3 2 1

Outfielder Al Oliver

CONTENTS

EXTRA INNINGS

G rowing up, Kenny Rogers worked on his family's straw-
berry farm. He did not have much time for anything else.
He finally began playing baseball during his senior year
of high school. He played right field. Two Texas Rangers
scouts attended one of his games. They were there main-
ly to watch another player. At the time, Rogers stood just 5-foot-9. He weighed
only 135 pounds. Yet he made an impression during warm-ups. "His first throw went
over the third baseman's head, and so did the second one," said Rangers scout
(and later general manager) Joe Klein. "His third throw went over the backstop. His
fourth hit the backstop. [Fellow scout] Joe [Marchese] said to me, 'We should sign
him in the 50th round as a pitcher.' We didn't even stay for the game."

The Rangers took Rogers in the 39th round of the 1982 Major League Baseball
(MLB) Draft. The young man had never seen an MLB game. He did not even know
how to throw a pitch. Rogers kicked around the minor leagues for seven years.
He won just 19 games. He may not have been joking when he said, "I believe the
only reason [Sarasota manager Tom Grieve] didn't release me the first couple of
years was that I brought the coaches strawberries from my father's farm."

Pitcher Kenny Rogers

ROBERT F. KENNEDY STADIUM,
WASHINGTON, D.C.,
SEPTEMBER 30, 1971

First baseman/outfielder Frank Howard

LEAVING ON A LOW NOTE

The Senators' final home game took place on
September 30, 1971. They faced the New York
Yankees. In the ninth inning, the Senators led,
7–5. But the stadium's security guards left early.
More than 10,000 fans walked in without paying.
They were angry that the team was relocating.
The first two Yankees hitters grounded out. At
that point, thinking the game was over, hundreds
of fans swarmed the field. They wanted souvenirs.
One grabbed first base and ran away. With
security personnel gone, clearing the field was
impossible. The Senators were forced to forfeit
the game to New York.

Rogers gradually improved. He earned a spot as a reliever on the Rangers' roster in 1989. Three years later, he led the major leagues with 81 appearances. In 1993, at the age of 28, he became a starter. He won 16 games. On July 28, 1994, the Rangers played the California Angels. Rogers took the mound. He retired the first three Angels hitters. The same thing happened in the next three innings. By then, his teammates had built up a 4–0 lead.

As the game went on, fans began to realize that no Angels player had reached first base. In the seventh inning, Rogers went to 3–2 counts on all three hitters. He retired each of them. Rogers emerged from the dugout to a wave of applause to start the eighth inning. There was an uneasy moment when the first Angels batter hit a sinking line drive. Thankfully, outfielder Juan González made the catch. Rogers struck out the next two batters.

"The crowd will grow crazy on every pitch here," said the TV announcer as the ninth inning began. The first California batter was infielder Rex Hudler. He stroked a low fly ball. Rookie outfielder Rusty Greer dove for it. He snagged it less than a foot from the ground, skidding to a stop. "I never thought he was going to get it," Rogers said. "I thought that ball was going to drop."

The next batter hit a ground ball to shortstop Esteban Beltré. Beltré's throw to first baseman Will Clark arrived in plenty of time. The third Angels hitter lofted a fly ball to center field. This time, Greer barely had to move to notch the final out.

Rogers had just thrown the 14th perfect game in MLB history. "It'll hit me in a couple of days just what's happened," Rogers said after the game. "I'm one of those guys now." Years later, Rogers looked back on his accomplishment. "It's unbelievable that I even got to the big leagues," he said. "My life would make a great movie. It has everything, mostly luck."

CAPITAL FLOPS

For many years, MLB was a tradition in Washington, D.C. The Washington Senators were a founding member of the American League (AL) in 1901. They won the World Series in 1924. But by the late 1930s, the Senators began to decline. Attendance waned. After the 1960 season, the franchise moved to Minneapolis. There it became the Minnesota Twins.

MLB quickly decided to establish another franchise in D.C. In 1961, a new Washington Senators team began playing. It was as bad as the first one! Owner Elwood R. Quesada was displeased. "Why should I be paying guys who aren't good enough to play in the major leagues?" he asked. One of the few who was "good enough" was slugging first baseman/outfielder Frank Howard. He joined the team in 1965. Thanks to his powerful hitting, teammates called him the "Capital Punisher." Howard became a four-time All-Star in Washington. But he could not carry the whole team on his broad shoulders.

The Senators compiled a string of losing seasons. In 1967, they rose to 6th place in the 10-team AL. But even with Howard's major-league-leading 44 home runs, they tumbled back into the cellar the following season. Legendary Boston Red Sox slugger Ted Williams was hired as manager in 1969. The team posted its first winning record. It finished the season 86–76. It was a 21-game improvement over the previous season. Williams earned the AL Manager of the Year award. Pitcher Dick Bosman recorded an AL-best 2.19 earned-run average (ERA). Howard

Catcher Paul Casanova

Manager Ted Williams

hit a career-high 48 homers. He led the team with 111 runs batted in (RBI). Senators fans began dreaming of bigger things.

Unfortunately, the team fell back under .500 in 1970. It closed 1971 with a dismal 63–93 record. Interest in the team fizzled. Attendance dwindled. Bob Short had purchased the franchise before the start of the 1969 season. He saw this loss of interest as an opportunity to head west. For the second time in 12 years, a D.C. baseball team was on the move.

MR. EVEN-STEVEN

Charlie Hough started his career with the Dodgers. He struggled at first. Then Dodgers scout Goldie Holt taught Hough how to throw a knuckleball. It became his signature pitch. Los Angeles used him primarily as a reliever. The Rangers made him a starter. In Texas, Hough averaged 14 wins and 225 innings pitched. In 1987, at the age of 39, he became the oldest pitcher to lead the majors in both starts (40) and innings pitched (285.1). Hough spent 13 seasons in the AL and 13 in the National League (NL). Twenty-two of those seasons were evenly divided between the Dodgers and the Rangers. The other four were split between the Chicago White Sox and the Florida Marlins. Overall, Hough won 216 games and lost 216.

CHARLIE HOUGH
PITCHER
RANGERS SEASONS: 1980–90
HEIGHT: 6-FOOT-2
WEIGHT: 190 POUNDS

TEXAS RANGERS

Shortstop Bucky Dent

OAKLAND-ALAMEDA
COUNTY COLISEUM,
OAKLAND, CALIFORNIA,
JULY 3, 1983

16

EXTRA-INNING BLOWOUT

The Rangers faced the Oakland Athletics. Texas took a 4–2 lead into the bottom of the ninth inning. Oakland battled back to tie the score. It remained knotted until the top of the 15th. Rangers shortstop Bucky Dent led off with a walk. A single and an intentional walk loaded the bases. Outfielder Bob Jones slapped a double to right field. Two runs scored. A wild pitch plated another run. That opened the floodgates. A total of eight hits, four walks, and an Oakland error resulted in 12 runs. Seven Rangers batted twice in the inning. The Rangers set an MLB record for runs scored in an extra inning. Texas won the game, 16–4.

MOVING OUT WEST

The Senators relocated to Arlington, Texas. It lies between the major cities of Dallas and Fort Worth. Short chose the new team name of Texas Rangers. It honored the legendary lawmen who had protected Texas settlers. The founding of that group of Rangers dated back to 1823.

The team posted an embarrassing 54–100 record in its first year in Texas. Howard was traded midseason. Williams retired. The Rangers shuffled through three different managers in 1973. They combined to lead the team to a miserable 57–105 record.

Things improved the following season. The team won 84 games. Outfielder Jeff Burroughs hit 25 homers and batted in 118 runs. He earned the Most Valuable Player (MVP) award. Pitcher Fergie Jenkins led the majors with 25 wins and 29 complete games. Jenkins said, "I didn't consider pitching to be work—I was having fun getting most hitters out in the major leagues."

For the remainder of the 1970s, the Rangers hovered near the middle of the AL West Division. The team's best performance of the decade came in 1977. It won 94 games that year. Five starters hit .284 or better. But Texas finished second in the AL West.

The new decade began the same way. Third baseman Buddy Bell batted a career-high .329 in 1980. Knuckleball ace Charlie Hough arrived in July. He became a fan favorite. But the team finished low in the standings. For the rest of the '80s, the Rangers continued their bumpy ride up and down the standings. They ended 1981 and 1986 in second place. But they never managed to top the AL West.

After two losing seasons, the franchise put together a formidable roster in 1989. Two rookies showed special promise. Third baseman Dean Palmer displayed sensational fielding. Outfielder Juan González swatted numerous home runs. Meanwhile, power hitter Rafael Palmeiro manned first base. Nolan Ryan, a native Texan, commanded the mound. The "Ryan Express" notched 16 wins. He recorded his 5,000th career strikeout along the way. Together, this mix of power and pitching carried the team to an 83–79 finish. More standouts emerged in 1990. Outfielder Rubén Sierra led the Rangers with 96 RBI. Kenny Rogers compiled 15 saves. The team finished 83–79 again. But it was 20 games behind the division-leading Oakland Athletics.

The highlight of the 1991 season came on May 1. Ryan hurled his seventh career no-hitter, three more than any other pitcher in MLB history. At 44, he became the oldest man to throw a no-hitter. Palmeiro, Sierra, and second baseman Julio Franco all hit .307 or better. Rookie catcher Iván Rodríguez thrilled fans with his bullet-like throws. The team put together its third straight winning season. But yet again, it remained out of the playoff picture.

The AL rearranged into three divisions in 1994. The Rangers remained in the AL West with three other teams. The shuffle marked the introduction of the Wild Card team. Unfortunately, a players' strike ended the season in August. The Rangers had been leading the division. But the playoffs were canceled.

Play started again in April 1995. The Rangers showcased a talented roster. Palmer posted a .336 average. Designated hitter Mickey Tettleton connected for 32 dingers. Rogers notched 17 wins. But the Rangers finished the season four and a half games shy of the playoffs.

Catcher Iván Rodríguez

IVÁN RODRÍGUEZ
CATCHER
RANGERS SEASONS:
   1991–2002, 2009
HEIGHT: 5-FOOT-9
WEIGHT: 205 POUNDS

GROWING INTO HIS NICKNAME

Iván Rodríguez signed with the Rangers at the age of 16. He stood 5-foot-7 and weighed 165 pounds. He kept growing. He became known as "Pudge." "I'm small and strong," he explained. After his rookie season, Rodríguez was an All-Star and Gold Glove winner for 10 years in a row. He earned the Silver Slugger award each year from 1994 through 1999. A year after becoming the youngest catcher to reach 1,000 hits, his batting average was .332 in 1999. He slammed 35 home runs and drove in 113 runs. He was voted MVP. His skill behind the plate was complemented by his powerful right arm, which routinely gunned down would-be base-stealers. Pudge entered the Hall of Fame in 2017.

BOOMING BATS

n 1996, the Rangers finished with a 90–72 record. They won the AL West title for the first time. González's 47 homers earned him MVP honors. Texas won the first game against the New York Yankees in the AL Division Series (ALDS). But it lost the next three by a combined total of four runs. The team's numbers fell the following season. It slumped back to third place.

The Rangers brought home the AL West crown in 1998 and 1999. Their bats were on fire. González slugged 45 homers in 1998. He also drove in a league-high 157 runs. He earned his second MVP award. "He is unbelievably strong and yet has such quick hands," Palmeiro said. "Even when he gets fooled [by a pitch], he can recover and then just snap his wrists—and the ball goes 450 feet." Unfortunately, the powerful Yankees swept the Rangers out of the playoffs both times. González left town before the 2000 season. The deflated Rangers sank to the bottom of the AL West.

Texas sent shock waves through the majors before the 2001 season. It signed free-agent shortstop Álex Rodríguez to a 10-year, $252-million contract. It was the largest in baseball history. "Our judgment is that Álex will break every record in baseball before he finishes his career," said owner Tom Hicks. "A-Rod" put his bat where his money was. He posted a .318 average and led the league with 52 home runs. He drove in 135 runs. But once again, the Rangers finished last. The next two seasons were nearly identical. Despite A-Rod's impressive performances, Texas remained mired in the basement.

Infielder Michael Young

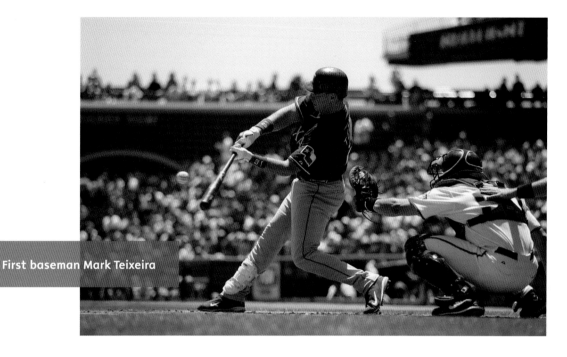

First baseman Mark Teixeira

In 2004, the Rangers made big changes. They traded Palmeiro. They also sent A-Rod to the Yankees. Texas received slugging second baseman Alfonso Soriano in return. His All-Star performance boosted the team to an 89–73 finish. Still, it was not enough for the playoffs.

The Rangers took third in the AL West the next two seasons. Several key players helped the team remain steady. Hank Blalock established himself as a solid third baseman. First baseman Mark Teixeira became one of baseball's biggest sluggers. He hit 43 homers and had 144 RBI in 2005. Michael Young excelled at shortstop.

By 2007, the Rangers slid back into the division cellar. They surged into second in 2008. The offense led the way. Second baseman Ian Kinsler enjoyed an All-Star season. Outfielder Josh Hamilton had a breakout season. He smacked 32 homers and led the league with 130 RBI. Texas led the majors in many offensive categories. But it finished 21 games behind the division-leading Los Angeles Angels of Anaheim.

First baseman Rafael Palmeiro

JUAN GONZÁLEZ
OUTFIELDER
RANGERS SEASONS:
1989–99, 2002–03
HEIGHT: 6-FOOT-3
WEIGHT: 175 POUNDS

JUAN GONE

Juan González grew up in Puerto Rico. He learned to hit using bottle caps, corks, and broomsticks. González could play any outfield position. He was one of the most feared hitters of his time. His nickname was "Juan Gone." He hit many balls into the outfield stands. He led the majors in home runs in 1992 and 1993 and was named MVP in 1996 and 1997. González drove in at least 102 runs in 7 of his Rangers seasons. He was traded in 1999. But Juan was not gone for good. He returned in 2002. As of 2019, he held team records for home runs (372) and RBI (1,180).

A COUPLE OF CLOSE CALLS

The Rangers started hot in 2009. They posted their first winning season in five years. But they finished in second place. The following year made up for any lingering disappointment. Young, right fielder Nelson Cruz, and designated hitter Vladimir Guerrero provided steady slugging. With 32 homers and a .359 average, Hamilton was named MVP. First-year closer Neftalí Feliz saved 40 games and won the Rookie of the Year award. The Rangers powered their way to a 90–72 record. They topped the AL West. They raced through the playoffs, toppling the Tampa Bay Rays and the Yankees. The team finally reached its first World Series. But it lost to the San Francisco Giants in five games. "We just got cold at the wrong time with the bats," said Hamilton.

The following season was even better. Texas won a franchise-record 96 games. It romped past the Rays and the Detroit Tigers in the playoffs. The Rangers faced the St. Louis Cardinals in the 2011 World Series. Texas won three of the first five games. It took a 7–5 lead into the bottom of the ninth inning of Game 6. But the Rangers could not hold on. The Cardinals won in the 11th inning to even the series. Then they cruised to a 6–2 victory in Game 7.

In 2012, the Rangers fell just short of the division title. They lost the Wild Card game to the Baltimore Orioles. Texas missed the playoffs the next two seasons. Bouncing back in 2015, the Rangers captured the division title. They faced the Toronto Blue Jays in the ALDS. They took both games in Toronto. But they lost the next two at home. Back in Toronto, the Rangers committed too many errors. The Blue Jays won, 6–3.

Right Fielder Nelson Cruz

BOMBS AWAY

The Rangers were set to play the Orioles in a doubleheader. Baltimore built a 3–0 lead. In the fourth inning, Texas catcher Jarrod Saltalamacchia hit a single. It drove in two runs. Infielder Ramón Vázquez followed with a three-run homer. In the sixth, Texas bats began booming. The team scored 25 runs during the final four innings. Saltalamacchia and Vázquez drove in seven apiece. Texas pounded 29 hits. It was the first time since 1897 that a team scored 30 runs. "This is something freaky," said outfielder Marlon Byrd. "You won't see anything like this again for a long, long time." Texas won the nightcap by a more modest score of 9–7.

ORIOLE PARK AT
CAMDEN YARDS,
BALTIMORE, MARYLAND,
AUGUST 22, 2007

TEXAS RANGERS

Texas improved to 95 wins in 2016. It easily topped the AL West. The Rangers again faced the Blue Jays in the ALDS. There was little suspense this time. Toronto opened the series with a 10–1 thrashing. The Rangers could not recover. The Blue Jays swept them in three games.

In 2017, Texas players struggled with injuries and sub-par performances. Still, the Rangers were in contention for a Wild Card slot until late in the season. They finished 78–84. Texas dropped to 67–95 in the following season. It climbed back to 78 wins in 2019. Afterward, first baseman Ronald Guzmán noted, "We don't take it as this year is over. We take it as this is the beginning of something great."

Since moving cross-country to Texas in 1972, the Rangers have proven that they have the same grit and steely determination as the lawmen of the Old West. They have worked hard to keep close to their competition. Although it took almost half a century for the team to reach its first World Series, the present-day Rangers are determined to secure their first world championship soon.

INDEX